MW01618192

This book is dedicated to my dear sister Beatrice, and Lewis.
With heartfelt thanks to Virginia.

And special thanks to:
Mark Gillmon for his love and help
John Davies for his initial inspiration
www.worldbicyclerelief.org

www.veronicalamond.com

Jojo's Wire Car

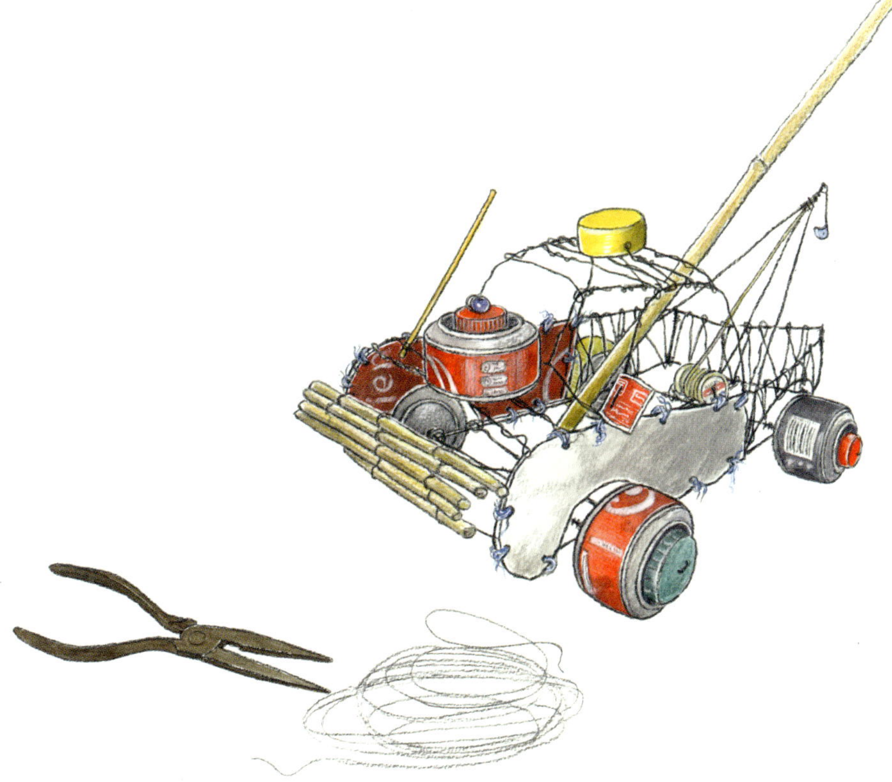

Written and illustrated by
Veronica Lamond

Jojo hardly had any time to play.

Every day he had to walk a long, long way to school, and a long, long way back home again.

Jojo's granny had a very sore foot so she couldn't walk properly.

Jojo had to help her with all the jobs around the home.

"Take this fruit, Jojo," said Granny. "Go and sell it by the roadside. We need money for your school books."

Jojo took an old cloth and laid out his little stall next to Yola.

The other children played happily in the street.
"I wish I had time to play with them," thought Jojo.

Hoot! Hoot! Mr Gilema drove up in his pick-up.

"Come on, children!" he called, pinning up a notice.

"We're running a Wire Car Competition!
Let's see how clever you are!"

The children were excited. "We must find some wire!" they shouted.

Wire Car Competition

For all children under 10 years old

****

First prize: 2 Years Free Schooling
Second prize: Bicycle
Third prize: Full Sports Kit

****

Judging will take place outside
Mulah Stores at 9am on 25 March

Good Luck Everyone!

When Jojo had sold all the fruit, he ran home. "I want to make a wire car, Granny!" he said.

"But you don't have enough time to find wire," she said. "Stop dreaming, my boy. The chickens need feeding and you must dig the vegetable garden."

"If I do my work quickly," thought Jojo, "there might be time to make a car as well!"

While he was feeding the hens, Jojo saw an old piece of wire poking out from under the hen house.

"I can use this!" he said, pulling it out.

By the time Jojo was able to go to the dump, he could find only one piece of wire …

… two empty drink cans and eight bent bicycle spokes.

All the other children had been there before him.

Wherever Jojo went, he saw everyone busily making their cars.

"Where can I get more wire from?" he asked Yola.
"Look what I've brought for you!" she said.

"Thank you very much!" said Jojo.

Musa was fixing the fence. While he was working, he dropped a roll of wire.

Then Musa came to buy some fruit.

"Will you let me have some wire if I give you this mango?" asked Jojo, knowing Granny would be very cross.

“Are you entering the competition too?” asked Musa. “Yes,” said Jojo. “But it’s difficult for me to find wire.”

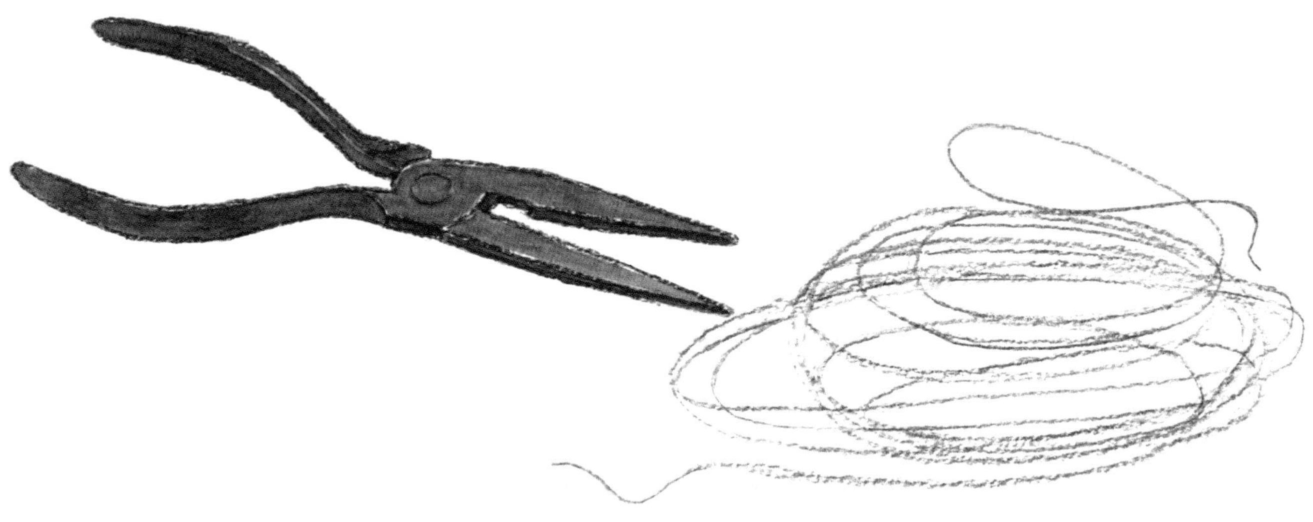

“Your granny needs the money for this mango,” Musa said. “But I know you work very hard to help her, so I’ll give you a piece of wire for your car and I’ll lend you my pliers!”

“Look Granny, I can start making my car!” said Jojo. “You’ll have to work at night, Jojo, when your homework and jobs are done,” she said.

The next day, on his way home from school, Jojo picked up old bottle tops and other bits of plastic that he could use.

That night Jojo made a chassis out of the bicycle spokes.
He cut up the cans and fitted the ends together to make the wheels.

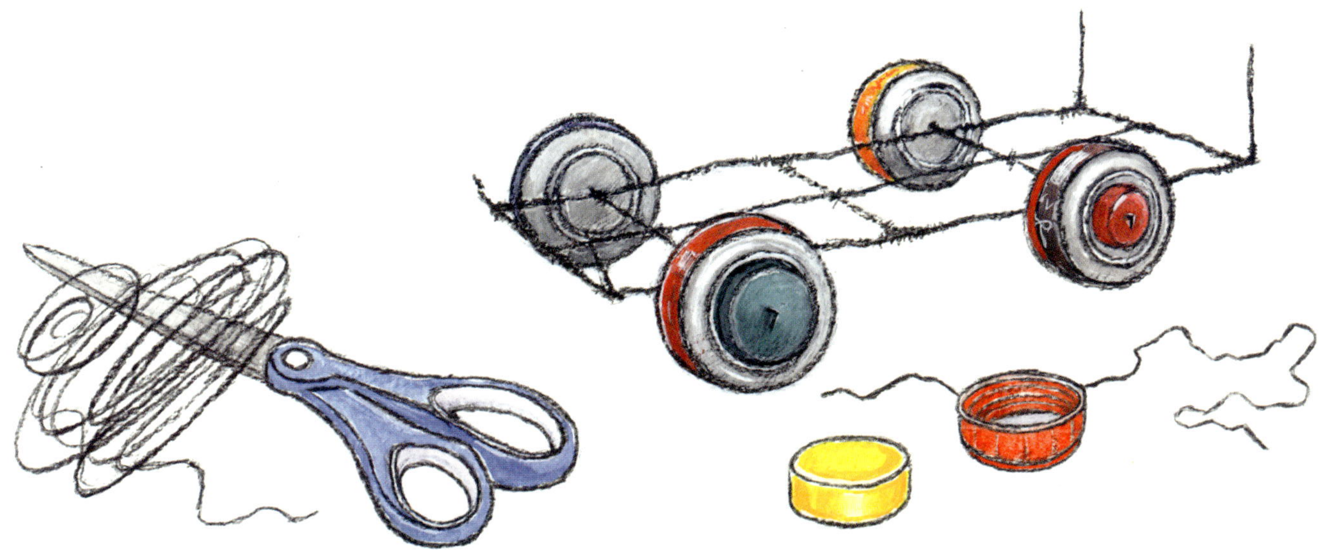

He used a block of wood and a stone to hammer and bend the coat hangers into two shapes for a truck.

"Time for bed now, Jojo," said Granny.

When Jojo got home from school the next day, he found Yola cleaning out the hen house for him.

“I’ve come to help you,” she said. “Judging day is tomorrow, so you don’t have much time to finish your car.”

Jojo worked late into the night. He wired on a grille made from sticks, twisting it on with Musa’s pliers.

Then Jojo fell fast asleep.

"Your mother would have been proud of you," whispered Granny, as she covered him up.

Jojo woke up early.

"You can do your jobs later," said Granny. "You must finish your car now."

Jojo worked quickly – he wired on a long handle, then he made a little crane with his last bits of wire.

"I need one more little piece to make a hook for the crane," he said. "But I've got no wire left!"

“Here,” said Granny, “take this.”

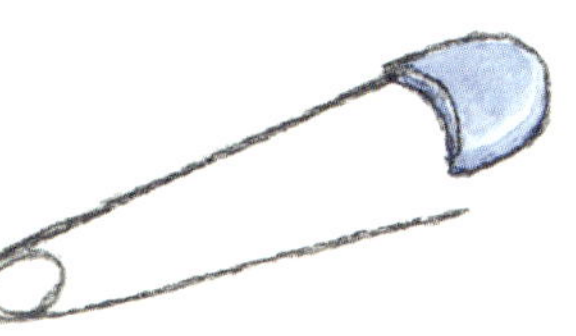

She took off the big safety pin from her apron and gave it to him to use.

It was perfect!

“Run now!” said Granny. “The other children have already gone to the competition. Yola will help me walk there.”

Everyone watched as the judges made up their minds.

"First prize goes to Chebe!" said Mr Gilema. "Two years free schooling for you!"

"Second prize goes to Jojo and he wins the bicycle!"

"Hooray for Jojo!" shouted Musa.

Now it was quick to get to school on the bike and Jojo was no longer tired when he got home.
He enjoyed his schoolwork and did very well in class.

"Look Granny, I can use my bike to help me with my jobs and earn money for my books!" he said.

...and there was also plenty of time to play!

Published by Struik Nature
(an imprint of Random House Struik (Pty) Ltd)
Reg. No. 1966/003153/07
Wembley Square, First Floor, Solan Road, Gardens, Cape Town
PO Box 1144, Cape Town, 8000 South Africa

Visit www.randomstruik.co.za and join the Struik Nature Club for updates, news, events and special offers.

First published in 2014 by Struik Nature

10 9 8 7 6 5 4 3 2 1

Printed and bound by Tien Wah Press (Pte) Ltd, Singapore

ISBN (African edition) 978 1 77584 117 3
ISBN (UK and European edition) 978 1 77584 147 0